YO-BZA-735

# Advanced Multitasking
## *Do More, Work Less, Be Happy*

## 2ʳᵈ Edition

## Michael Sanders, MA

# DEDICATION

I would like to dedicate this book to my family, friends and business associates who helped me understand how task management really works. After many years of formal management education, countless corporate courses, and a wide variety of business association certifications, it was my friends and associates who really taught me how to manage tasks … and a Roman from 43 BC.

# CONTENTS

# PREFACE

This book is about multitasking and what I learned in my investigation, analysis, and work on the topic. Although I had thought just the opposite, I learned my life was actually falling apart and multitasking did not exist. It was consoling to read the words by a Roman poet who shattered my multitasking illusion in the first place, "It is better to learn late than never" (Syrus, 43 BC). I hope the information presented in this book helps you as it has me.

After learning more about tasking and the brain, I now spend a lot of time determining not only what I cannot do, but the difference between what I want to do and what I can do. I am very stingy with my time now. My new habit of task minding and guarding time creates the space for me to do the things I really want to do, the important things, and helps me resist my compulsion to say yes to all things shiny, brought on by emotion and carelessness. Suffice to say, we should all strive to do the best we can, the most we can. This was no better said than by Don Juan in Carlos Castaneda's Teachings of Don Juan:

> "When one has fulfilled those requisites, there are no mistakes to account. Under such conditions, one's acts lose the blundering quality of a fool's acts. If such a person fails or suffers a defeat, that person has lost only a battle, and there will be no regrets over that." (Castaneda, 1968)

I must also own up to something. There is not an original thought in this book. All of the material is from information available to all (see the many references). And some of my references are over 50 years old! This research has been around for a while. My meager contribution was to simply arrange the information in a unique way and formulate a model to make sense of sound and effective tasking to even a slow learner like me.

Finally, I believe we are all students for life and learn together. And I sincerely thank you for reading this book and urge you to contact me directly with any comments or suggestions to make the material better. Please let me know what you think.

My very best to you.

**Mailing Address**:

Mike Sanders
2913 El Camino Real, No. 432,
Tustin, Ca. 92782

**Email**: mike@mike-sanders.com

**Email:** info@advanced-multitasking.com

**LinkedIn**: http://www.linkedin.com/in/mikesanders1

**Website**: www.Advanced-Multitasking.com (downloads)

# 1

# A SEPARATE REALITY

## Could I be the greatest multitasker, ever?

### Multitasking Par Excellence!

A few years ago I was a technical writer in Los Angeles working on several contracts at the same time. I really liked consulting because it gave me a lot of freedom and it made me a lot of money. The catch was to never be out of work. Although four of my friends in the same field charged a much higher hourly rates (some 50% higher), I made more money than they did because I always had work.

My business model was simple - charge a nominal hourly rate but have continuous work, and lots of it. So a big part of my time was spent digging up more jobs, even when I had one, or even more than one.

I was good at it. At one point in time I actually had four contracts at the same time – two were fulltime! And during this time, it was not unusual for me to visit several of these job sites on the same day.

Job locations stretched over a 100 miles in Southern California from Ventura County through Los Angeles County and down into South Orange County. Although having multiple deliverables on the same day was not unusual for me, the traveling I had to do on one particular day resulted in a life-changing event.

On this day, I needed to be and work onsite at all four job locations; be on two, one-hour, conference calls at the same time; prepare a presentation for one of my jobs; eat lunch (a banana); and prepare and deliver a complex analysis for another job. And I did it all! At the end of this trek, and while basking in victory in my car in an Irvine, California parking lot, I felt not only I was a good multitasker, but an incredible one. On that day, I decided to find out more about multitasking, why I was so incredibly good at it, and how to share my gift with the world!

The result of my investigation was a dose of humbling self-reflection and truth. It was gut-wrenching and redeeming, leading to a new view of work that changed my life - no, saved my life. Here is my story.

# Multitasking does not exist. I can prove it.

## Multitasking – Illusion or Reality?

My multitasking investigation began with a dose of honest self-reflection. Since I had been keeping a detailed planner of my daily tasks for over 20 years, I decided to prove my multitasking prowess by measuring my gift with personal metrics over the past year leading up to the date of my "super" multitasking event.

These metrics were:

- Task Loading (current working tasks)

- Weekly Overtime (hours worked over 40)

- Health (weight fluctuation)

- Happiness (fun time, doing things to be happy)

- Relationships (with key people in my life)

- Task Completions (on a weekly basis)

## Tasking Metrics

The results of my 12-month tasking analysis were astonishing.

- **Task Loading.** At the height of my multitasking prowess, I had twice as many weekly tasks on my plate compared to the year previous. I was very proud of this!

- **Weekly Overtime.** I had effectively doubled my weekly overtime, going from an average of 7 hours per week to over 15. Some weeks approached 30. I was extremely proud of this!

- **Health.** I had gained over 40 pounds over the past year and was not in very good physical condition. I realized this after seeing notes about not feeling or sleeping well often, as well notations on getting regular colds and flues. This worried me a bit.

- **Happiness.** There were almost no fun entries in my planner during the second half of the year. I was not doing any of the things I loved to do any more. There was little time for fun and when I had time, I was tired and chose to rest. This made me question my priorities. Was I working to live or living to work?

- **Relationships.** There were clear signs of progressively strained relationships. Others had actually made notes in my planner indicating these poor relationships at work and at home. My notations and those of others were actually shocking to me as I re-read them. This made me sad.

- **Task Completions.** The most shocking fact of all was I was only completing half as many tasks as I had a year prior. This was in stark contrast to having twice as many weekly tasks in plate currently. This horrified me.

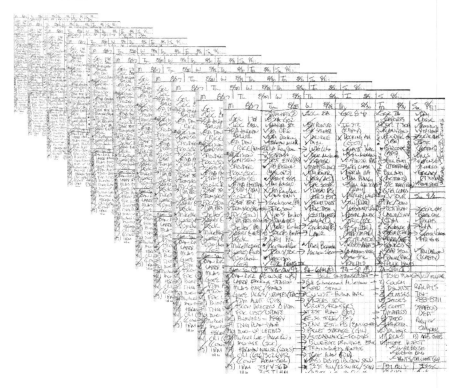

**12 Months of My Personal Planner**

The fact is I would have bet everything I owned on having become a more effective, healthier, happier, and grounded multitasker over that 12 months. But the hard truth was just the opposite. I was failing in every possible measure: in my work, in my health, in fun activities and in my relationships.

The truth hurt. Frankly, I realized I was failing in my life. So I decided to find out more about the topic of multitasking, about what had happened to me, and how to turn things around. What I found was that multitasking does not exist.

## A Roman Gave Us Good Advice

To find out more about my poor tasking performance, I decided to research the topic on the Internet. So I entered the word "multitasking" in my web browser and clicked Enter. One of the first bits of information I retrieved was a quote from a Roman philosopher, Publilius Syrus (FixQuotes), from 43 BC.

Syrus was a Latin writer of maxims, and very successful in the 1st century BC. Although Syrian born, he was brought to Italy as slave, but eventually freed and educated due to his great intellect. In one of his many maxims, Syrus cautioned us, *"To do two things at once is to do neither"* (FixQuotes).

Syrus' maxim was unsettling to me. It either meant multitasking is inefficient and does not work well or does not exist at all. My view was I could indeed do two things at the same time, and I did it all the time! But the Romans were pretty good at what they did back then. After all, they <u>had</u> conquered the world. So I opened my mind to more information in my Internet research. And, yes, a ton of information came tumbling in. Research spanning 50 years had been done on multitasking and its conclusions were not good news for us multitaskers.

So I wanted to know if multitasking even existed. And the answer I got was clear, it does not exist (reference). At least, multitasking does not exist in terms of our definition. So if multitasking does not exist, if we cannot do more than one thing at the same time, what are we doing when we think we are multitasking?

## Task Switching

The answer is we are actually task switching (Mayr & Kliegl, 2000; Yeung & Monsell, 2003). We are switching from task to task, back and forth, forward and back, and sometimes many times a minute. But we are never doing more than one thing at the same time.

Research by Frederick Luskin, senior consultant in Health Promotion at Stanford University and Professor of Clinical Psychology at the Institute of Transpersonal Psychology, supports the premise of multiple task switching (Dvorsky, 2007; Hawthorne, 2009). Luskin concluded human beings have approximately 60,000 thoughts per day.

And of these many thoughts, over 90 percent are repetitive and 80 percent negative (Comaford, 2012). We can classify a majority of these many thoughts as task switching simply because they move us off the task at hand. Our thoughts are serious business.

## The Origins of Multitasking

Where did the term multitasking come from? Let us go back to our definition of multitasking, "doing more than one thing at the same time." This is actually the second definition of multitasking. If we investigate the term a bit further, the most common and formal definition we find goes something like this, "the concurrent performance of several jobs by a computer" (Merriam-Webster, 2014). Multitasking comes from the computer industry. The logic in using it for people goes something like this. We compare our brain to a computer's brain, or central processing unit.

This allows us to equate our brain's functionality to that of a computer. And since, according to the definition, a computer can perform several jobs concurrently (concurrent performance of several jobs by a computer), we should be able to do the same.

But here is the catch; computers do not really perform several jobs at the same. They are simply task switching. Computers perform preemptive tasking (time slicing or time sharing) as their form of multitasking. Here a computer executes a part of one program, then switches to another, and then returns to the first program: task switching.

The reason computers appear to be doing pure multitasking is because they switch tasks at extremely high speeds. This high-speed switching has the appearance of concurrent operation or "concurrently performing several jobs at the same time."

# We are not computers.

But unlike our computers, we are not very good at task switching (Altmann & Gray, 2002). There are very good reasons for this which lies at the root of why our attempts at multitasking, or task switching, do not work out well for us. Research shows there is a serious problem with frequent and prolonged task switching (Avery-Snell, 2007). It not only does not work well from an efficiency standpoint, it can be very harmful to our brain over time (Mayr & Kliegl, 2000).

The bottom line is the Romans gave us some very good advice: "To do two things at once is to do neither."

# 2

# THE PROBLEM:
# TASK SWITCHING

What we've lost, above all
is stopping points, finish
lines, and boundaries.

Like we discussed earlier, task switching does not generally work well for us. Unlike computers, humans tend to emotionally cling to tasks. This clinging causes a host of problems that can end in cognitive damage to the brain.

In a Harvard Business Review article, Tony Schwartz cites the following:

"It's not just the number of hours we're working, but also the fact we spend too many continuous hours juggling too many things at the same time. What we've lost, above all is stopping points, finish lines, and boundaries. Technology has blurred them beyond recognition. Wherever we go, our work follows us, on our digital devices, ever insistent and intrusive. It's like and itch we can't resist scratching, even though scratching invariably makes it worse." (Schwartz, 2012)

## The Multitasking Illusion – The Task Monkeys!

Attempting to multitask is not good for us. What we think we are doing when multitasking is shown on the timeline in Figure 1 below. We begin by engaging in a single task, shown below as Task 1. Time goes by and we engage another task, Task 2, but we think we can continue to work on Task 1 in the background. You might say we believe there is some sort of task monkey working quietly on the original Task 1 while we are fully engaged on Task 2. Then we engage more task monkeys to work on Tasks 1 and 2 in the background as we fully engage Task 3. The process continues onto Task 4 and Task 5 as shown below.

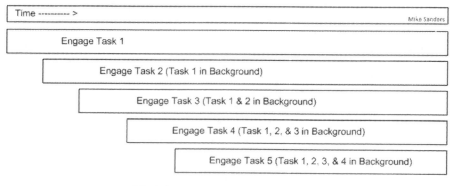

**Multitasking - We Think**

However, the reality is we have not fully engaged any tasks in this model. We simply work on them at some capacity of attention. Alas, there are no monkeys.

## The Multitasking Reality - Task Switching

Multitasking, as we have defined it, does not actually exist. The timeline below is a depiction of the real tasking process - task switching. In a typical task performance cycle, as shown on the timeline below, after engaging Task 1, we "switch "to Task 2. The problem is we still have residue thinking linking us to Task 1, and may even switch back to Task 1 periodically.

Following the timeline below, we then formally switch back to Task 1. But we have not fully switched, as we have residue thinking linking us back to Task 2 as well as the original Task 1 in our conscious brain.

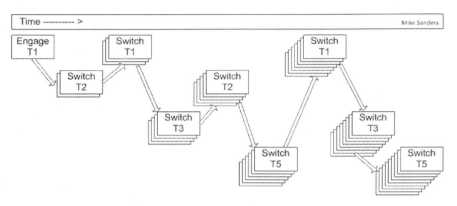

## Multitasking - We Are Not

As we continue to switch tasks on the timeline above, residue thoughts linking to previous tasks, as well as actual switchbacks to previous tasks blur our focus and our ability to perform optimally. Our general thinking now begins to skew, and goes off mark. By the end of a days-worth of undisciplined task switching, we can become submerged, even overwhelmed, in a cloud of task residue resulting in mistakes, miscues, degraded performance, and brain freezing. Emotionally, this can result confusion, anxiety, and depression. Task failure is not far behind.

## Tasking Under the Influence (TUI)

I refer to task thought residue from improper task switching as "tasking under the influence" or TUI (Meyer & Kieras, 1997a; Meyer & Kieras, 1997b). Thinking back at the illusion of multitasking, again, there are no task monkeys working on tasks in the background, only intermittent and ineffective attention switching. This switching can happen erratically and often, producing incomplete thinking, poor logic, loss of focus, mistakes, anxiety and confusion. It also extracts a high price physiologically within our brain (Estes, 1955). The conclusion is we want to avoid TUI.

## Task Switching Losses

Done improperly, task switching can have several harmful effects. For instance, over time, task switching can actually impair the brain's functioning physiologically. Synapses can begin to misfire due to jumbled circuits (Psychology Matters; Rogers & Monsell, .1995). When the brain's circuits are jumbled, thoughts and logic become flawed and incomplete. Perception is skewed, and even memory loss can occur. This thought-jammed condition, ironically affecting most overachievers, can result in the exact opposite of the intended result - significant mistakes, inevitable loss of productivity, and under-achievement.

It is ironical multitasking is the very reason overachievers can produce the exact opposite of their desired result - poor performance and ultimate failure. The costs of undisciplined task switching can be high. As a matter of fact, attempting to multitask through undisciplined task switching can nullify all work performed in any given day from four factors. These factors include the switching gap, task engagement lag, engagement and performance mistakes, and lack of proper of task prioritization.

## The Gap

Lost time in the tasking switching gap is the result of a simple brain response, or initial non-response, to the switch. That is, for a small period of time after switching to a task nothing at all is happening in the brain, hence the term "gap" (Smith, 2001). The length and depth of the task switching gap are affected by several factors: health, workload, work stress, and task complexity. These factors all affect the total time lost in the gap.

## The Lag

Lost time from the lag or boot up into the task can be significant is the result of several factors: task complexity, task frequency and distractions. The better prepared we are to engager our tasks after a switch results in less lost time booting up into the task (Smith, 2001).

## Performance Mistakes

Lost time from mistakes come from not engaging the task with the proper information. This can happen in many ways. For example, we may be working on one task with mistaken assumptions and guidelines from another. Or we may make critical mistakes from lack of focus or lack of information (Rogers & Monsell, 1995).

## Lack of Task Prioritization

Lost time from lack of appropriate prioritization may be the most serious risks to effective performance (Posen, 2012). Although we may work very competently and extremely hard, if we are working on tasks not needed or instead of tasks needed, our ultimate performance may be totally insignificant.

## Cumulative Time Loss from Task Switching

It has been estimated the switching gap can result in 5% loss, the engagement lag 20% loss, performance mistakes 25% loss, and poor or lack of task prioritization 50% loss in time (Altmann, 2004a; Altmann, 2004b; Altmann & Gray, 2002; Fagot, 1994; Kieras, Meyer, Ballas, & Lauber, 2000; Meyer & Kieras, 1997a; Kieras, Meyer, Ballas, & Lauber, 2000; Meyer & Kieras, 1997b).

- Lost time from the task switching gap (~5%)

- Lost time from the lag or booting time in the initial task engagement (~20%)

- Lost time from mistakes made in bad assumptions and processing errors (~25%)

- Lost time from poor or lack of prioritization, working on the wrong task (~50%)

The conclusion is this: we can be 100% ineffective on any given day from undisciplined task switching (Jarrehult, 2012).

# 3

# EFFECTIVE TASK SWITCHING

To become effective in task switching, we must understand its barriers and enablers. That is, if we know what to avoid and what to embrace, our task switching efforts will be much more successful – engaging and de-engaging.

## Task Switching Barriers

There are three barriers to effective task switching: switch frequency, task complexity, and distractions (Yeung & Monsell, 2003).

### Switching frequency

Switching frequency is a key barrier in effective task switching. This is because the more often we switch tasks, the more task thought residue we retain from the previous tasks. Frequent task switching is becoming more and more problematic since the attention distractions have increased exponentially in recent years.

For instance, smart phones beckon us to continually check for emails, tweets, Facebook, LinkedIn, news, alerts, scores, and so on. Additionally, tasks we perform at work have become increasingly switchable with the greater use of personal computers and matrixed tasking. This means for us to focus and switch tasks properly, we need to be stingy about sharing our attention with the likes of our smart phones and the many other options for distractions. The more often we switch tasks add to the difficulty in task switching.

### Task Complexity

Task complexity is another key barrier in effective task switching (Yeung & Monsell, 2003). Tasks today have become much more complex than they were even ten years ago. I remember hiring into a company 10 years ago and being on the job working within an hour. Today, my employer requires at least a week of training before you can complete a timesheet or vacation request. The workplace and our personal lives are significantly more complex. This higher complexity translates into more cognitive decision making on even the simplest of tasks – like creating a timesheet or completing a vacation request. Switching between complex tasks is significantly more difficult than switching between simple tasks.

## *Distractions*

Distractions round out the barriers to effective task switching. Distractions include physical distractions such as noise, lighting, phones, email, smart phones, texting, interruptions, bosses, and meetings. Body distractions include hunger, headaches, illnesses such as colds and flu, confusion, and injury. But the most significant distractions are unquestionably emotional. Emotional distractions include anger, fear, jealousy, envy, pride, anxiety, insecurity, unhappiness, happiness, and love. All distractions are barriers to effective task switching because they dampen our cognitive ability.

## Task Switching Enablers

Effective task switching is enabled by several factors. These factors include cognitive preparation (analysis), task prioritization, creating task queues (Gopher, Armony, & Greenspan, 2000), properly engaging tasks, properly de-engaging tasks, reducing task load, and obtaining feedback to improve the tasking process. Task switching enablers are discussed in depth in Chapter 5 – Cognitive Thinking.

# 4

# ADVANCED MULTITASKING

## Advanced multitasking is not multitasking.

Advanced multitasking is in fact the process of mindfully tasking switching and managing those switches throughout the day. The model below should the overall process. The process begins with proper conscious thinking - that is, putting your thinking in the correct brain. Next, you prioritize all tasks, personal and business.

Once armed with task priorities, you create task queues for all tasks. As you begin tasking, you will engage and de-engage tasks rather than reactively switch tasked without discipline or preparation. As you perform your tasks, consider them for possible deletion, delegation, transfer or reduction in scope (shaving). To monitor tasking progress, continually obtain feedback from others and incorporate changes in our tasking process.

The model below is a representation of the advanced multitasking process, which is actually not multitasking at all.

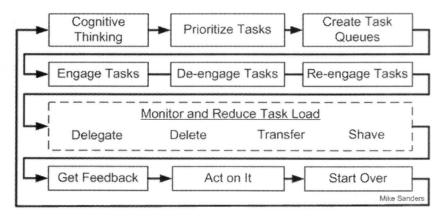

**Advanced Multitasking Model**

## Prepare for Cognitive Thinking

Chapter 5 discusses our four cognitive brains and how to access your higher thinking. This chapter includes discussions on the Hawthorne Effect, personal planners, visualization, and tapping into the non-conscious brain.

## List and Prioritize Tasks, Validate Priorities

Chapter 6 discusses the process to list and prioritize tasks. It also describes the corollary benefits to prioritizing using self-management and the need to pulse business and personal stakeholders.

## Create Task Queues, Engage and De-engage

Chapter 7 discusses task queues, task engagement, and task de-engagement. Each element is a key factor in effective, disciplined task management.

## Monitor and Reduce Task Load

Chapter 8 discusses monitoring and reducing your task load. Using four tools: deleting, delegating, transferring and shaving scope. You need eliminate all unnecessary tasks and distractions to focus on tasks that support your higher goals, the ones that matter.

## Get Feedback on Tasking and Act on It

Chapter 9 discusses getting much needed feedback on your tasking progress and then acting on that feedback. There is no greater mistake than to ask for and obtain feedback and then not act on it. Non-action has two problems: missed opportunities and insults to those who took the time to offer help. Act on it.

## Why Advanced Multitasking?

Chapter 10 discusses the advanced multitasking process and recommends steps to use and reinforce this new approach to tasking.

## Drink More Water

Chapter 11 discusses physiological brain maintenance, or drinking an ample supply of good-quality water daily. Properly brain hydration supports better and more focused thinking and decision making. Water is also good for you!

## What's Next

Chapter 12 discusses how to use multitasking and next steps in the process.

# 5

# CONGITIVE THINKING

Optimizing your performance begins with awareness of your cognitive thinking. Proper cognitive thinking must be considered when we are planning high-level task performance, prioritizing tasks, and when we are actually performing tasks With respect to prioritizing tasks, we must consider our high-level goals, available resources, and the time we have to perform tasks. To do our best, we need know which cognitive brain we are working in and ensure it is the correct one for the task at hand.

## What is a cognitive brain?

In fact, you have four cognitive brains, or what we can define as levels of cognitive thinking (Waller, 2004). These four levels include our physical, emotional, analytical, and non-conscious brains as shown in the diagram below.

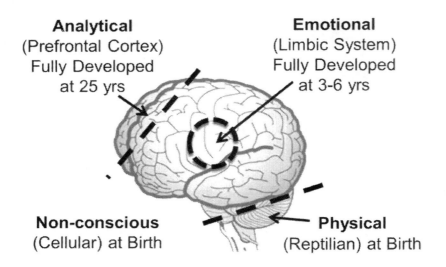

**Analytical**
(Prefrontal Cortex)
Fully Developed
at 25 yrs

**Emotional**
(Limbic System)
Fully Developed
at 3-6 yrs

**Non-conscious**
(Cellular) at Birth

**Physical**
(Reptilian) at Birth

**The Four Cognitive Brains**

## The Physical Cognitive Brain

The physical brain is like a bodyguard always watching out for us, continually scanning the environment for any threats. This brain, often referred to as the reptilian brain, also decides whether you will move into the fight or flight posture. The thinking, or analytical brain, is much too slow for such an important task as survival and to deal with immediate threats. The physical, reptilian brain is fully developed at birth.

## The Emotional Cognitive Brain

The emotional brain, or limbic system and also referred to as the mammalian brain, is a set of brain structures including the hippocampus, amygdala, anterior thalamic nuclei, septum, limbic cortex and fornix. The limbic brain supports a variety of functions including emotions, behavior, motivation, long term memory, and olfaction. The limbic system is not fully developed at birth. It becomes fully developed between the ages of 3 and 6 years old. Then, fully developed, we retain the characteristics of our emotional brain for the rest of our lives. As adults, emotionally we are essentially a group of 3 to 6 year-olds, no matter our age!

## The Analytical Cognitive Brain

The analytical brain (or prefrontal cortex) is charged with planning complex cognitive behavior, personality expression, decision making and social behavior (Gerhand, 1999). The main activity of the prefrontal cortex is to create thoughts and actions in agreement with our internal goals.

The prefrontal cortex is also one of the last parts of the brain to mature. Key functions of the prefrontal cortex include:

- Focusing
- Organizing thoughts
- Problem solving
- Foreseeing and judging consequences of behavior
- Predicting the future
- Strategizing and planning
- Balancing short-term rewards with long term goals
- Shifting and adjusting behavior situationally
- Controlling impulses and delaying gratification
- Modulating intense emotions
- Inhibiting inappropriate behavior

- Initiating appropriate behavior
- Processing multiple streams of complex information

The prefrontal cortex provides the capacity to perform good judgment in difficult situations. But just because the prefrontal cortex is developed does not mean we use it. Daily news of serious ethics and moral misjudgments are quick reminders that major decisions are not necessarily derived from the advanced thinking of the prefrontal cortex. Research indicates the prefrontal cortex is not fully developed until the approximate age of 25.

## The Hawthorne Effect

The Hawthorne Effect refers to the tendency of some people to work harder and perform better when they participate in an experiment. Behavior may change due solely to the attention received from observers rather than changes in task variables (Clark, 2010).

The Hawthorne Effect was first proposed from the results of experiments conducted in the 1920s and 1930s at the Hawthorne works electric company in Chicago. The company had commissioned research to find see if there was a relationship between productivity and worker environment (Dictionary of Sociology, 1998).

The focus of the Hawthorne studies was to determine if increasing and decreasing the amount of light workers received had an effect on productivity. Although employee productivity appeared to increase due to the light variations, it decreased when the experiment ended. Observers suggested productivity increases were attributable to the effect of the attention received from the observer team and not due changes to the lighting. As a result, the Hawthorne Effect was defined as a short-term improvement in performance caused by simply observing workers (Clark, 2010).

Making decisions of high-level goals and life direction are much richer and long lasting when made using your higher cognitive brain. Your analytical brain is much more able to make unbiased, deep-thinking, ethical, and healthy life decisions. The only question is, "how do I consciously access this higher intelligence?" Create an Inner CEO.

## Defeating the Hawthorne Effect - The Inner CEO

Although the focus of the Hawthorne studies was to determine if, by increasing and decreasing the amount of light workers were exposed to, productivity would be affected. However, the conclusion of the study was productivity was related to attention (Economist, 2008). And even though productivity increased due to the lighting changes, it actually went back to normal at after the experiment ended. Researchers suggested the productivity increase was due to attention the workers received from the research team and not due lighting changes in the experiment. The real issue is how do we defeat the Hawthorne Effect in our everyday lives – that is, how can we improve productivity when not observed?

The concept of creating an Inner CEO (Chief Operating Officer) offers a solution defeating the Hawthorne Effect –

or the natural dissipation of performance from lack of observation (Rubenstein, Mayer, & Evans, 2001). The premise is we all need someone or something inside of us to observe our actions and decisions to keep our performance at maximum and on track with our higher goals and needs. Our prefrontal cortex (or analytical brain) is an excellent candidate for this important task. The question is how can we create and access this Inner CEO regularly and effectively?

## Using a Personal Planner

One way to defeat the Hawthorne Effect with an Inner CEO is through the purposeful use of a personal planner. A personal planner, maintained daily and including both business and personal tasks, goals, thoughts and events acts as an Inner CEO as an overseer of our lives. A personal planner allows us to keep ourselves honest to our higher self. An example of a personal planner layout is shown below showing left and right pages. In this type of planner, one creates their own template each week with a "Week at a Glance" view.

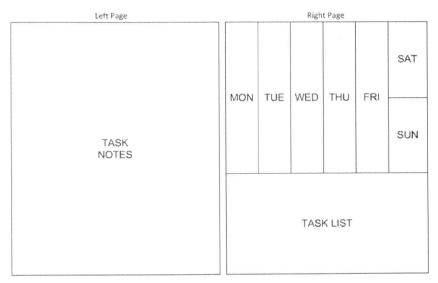

## Week-at-a-Glance Personal Planner System

Using this type of week-at-a-glance personal planner system, first purchase a durable, quad-ruled, sewn-backed, hard cover book. Next, create index pages in front of the planner by entering frequently-used information such as addresses, phone numbers, birthdays, key events, lists, and procedures. You can also tape reduced-size pages of reference information. Next, create your right page weekly days for about three months. Create Notes on the left pages and Reference pages at the back of planner with reduced-size copies of reference documents as tasks dictate during the year.

Build your planner task list and schedule a week ahead of the start of each week. First, list all tasks in the Task List area. Prioritize these tasks. Enter the tasks in the appropriate day above and place a dot to the left of the task in the task list area. As tasks are completed, place a checkmark to the left of the task entry in both the Day column and Task List.

If tasks are not completed, move them to another day and place a right arrow to the left of the original task entry. If a task is deleted or transferred, place an X to the left of the task. In the case of a transfer, not who received the task in the Notes page. Do not strike through any entry. Note if tasks are continually being moved without acting on them, they are candidates for deletion, delegation, transfer or reduction in scope.

In the Notes area, enter task notes and reference data, paste reduced-sized drawings, business cards, and memos. To help categorize notes, draw boxes around them and label them.

To be an effective Inner CEO, the personal planner must be used continually and updated with complete information on tasks, priorities, and long-term goals. This self-observation both keeps us honest to our long term goals and accesses our analytical brain, our prefrontal cortex.

Tracking tasks has a calming and powerful effect on our lives. By prioritizing our tasks while in our analytical brain, both for personal and professional tasks, we are able to control our future at a high level. Using a planner allows us to crystalize our day, reflect on our day, and understand what we need to give up as well as do to get what is important in our lives. What this really means is we cannot do everything and as a result have to make important choices continually. The Mental CEO allows those choices to be informed and in our best interests.

## Accessing the Prefrontal Cortex - MicroMeditation

Another way to access our prefrontal cortex (or higher brain) for higher level thinking and planning is to perform visualization. When visualizing, you are squarely accessing your prefrontal cortex. MicroMeditation is a good way to perform visualization in a very short time – just 60 seconds! The six steps below are done in 10-second increments ending with your answer to a very important  question, "what do you want?" The key is to answer this important question in just one or two words. Follow the steps below (ten seconds each):

1. Breathe in, and exhale.
2. Breathe in, and exhale.
3. Breathe in, and visualize a banana.
4. Breathe in, and now peel the banana.
5. Breathe in, and take a bite of the banana.
6. Breathe and answer "What do you want?"

Everything you do on your task list should fall under and be consistent with your answer to "what you want." Now you are ready for task prioritization.

# The Non-conscious Cognitive Brain

Our non-conscious, cognitive brain is composed of our nervous system and cellular intelligence matrix. The non-conscious brain carries a vast amount of thought power. Our bodies and composed of over 70 trillion cells (Shier, Butler, & Lewis, 2013), and our nervous system monitors and controls the behavior of the vast functions of these cells within and between them in our body – and it does this 24 hours a day. As a matter of fact, our cellular intelligence is so vast each one of our 70 trillion cells contains the blueprint (DNA) to create our entire human body (Alvino, 2007).

Research estimates our bodies are bombarded with approximately 40 million bits of information per second. Our non-conscious, cognitive nervous system processes about 11 million bits of this information per second. Yet our conscious brain can process only 40 bits per second (Wechsler, 2006). Correct, just 40 bits of information per second. If we compare 11 million to 40, the answer is clear: it would be a good thing if we could tap into the super-intelligence of the behind the scenes, non-conscious cognitive body (Koch, 2009).

As discussed previously, making decisions on high-level goals and life direction are much richer and long lasting when using your higher brain. Your non-conscious brain allows you to make more unbiased, deep-thinking, ethical, and healthy life decisions. The only question is, "how do I consciously access this higher intelligence?"

## Access Your Non-Conscious Brain

Inhabiting your body allows you to access your non-conscious brain. This includes your nervous system and the vast cellular intelligence in your entire body. Your body is constructed with over 70 trillion cells and each cell has intelligence. Additionally, your nervous system controls a vast, almost immeasurable matrix of networking and functioning amongst these cells. The goal here is to inhabit your body and tap into this intelligence. The procedure below will help you do this. Do this procedure before high level task planning and task analysis.

- Sit in an upright, relaxed position, close your eyes.
- Regulate your breathing in deep, even cycles.
- Visualize your feet and breathe air into them.
- Visualize your legs and breathe air into them.
- Visualize your hips and breathe air into them.
- Visualize your stomach and breathe air into it.
- Visualize your chest and breathe air into them.
- Visualize your shoulders and breathe air into them.
- Visualize your arms and breathe air into them.
- Visualize your neck and breathe air into it.
- Visualize your head and breathe air into it.
- Visualize your feet and breathe air into them.
- Open your eyes, look, inhabit your motionless hand.
- Close your eyes, visualize, inhabit your motionless hand.

- Repeat this visualization to inhabit your feet, nose, and ears.

- Now inhabit your entire body.

Your conscious brain is now supercharged with cellular intelligence and is ready to do advanced planning, analysis, and most importantly, task prioritizing.

# LIST AND PRIORITIZE TASKS

Making decisions about task priorities are better made when thinking is calm and based in logics and foresight – the prefrontal cortex. Priorities should not be made at the time of a task switch. This is because our thoughts and logic steer into our emotional brain during times of stress and in the anxiety of the moment (Sohn & Anderson, 2003).

When we are in the mix of task performance, it is not a good time to make key decisions about the most important tasks to work on. It is much better to plan for task switching by prioritizing your tasks ahead of time.

## List All Tasks – Personal and Business

Take some time to list all your tasks both personal and business. If you are have trouble coming up with a complete list, check with key stakeholders in your life including your manager, co-workers, vendors, clients, family, friends, and spouse. List all tasks together and begin determining which tasks are most important, next in importance, and last in importance. Consider using the ABC method. That is, place adjacent to each task an A for high importance, B for medium importance and C for low importance.

## Prioritize Your Tasks

Now task the master list and organize the tasks in order or priority, or importance. Place all the A's together and organize them from most important to least important. Do the same with the B's and the C's. When you are done, you will have a long list of tasks, and inventory, of what you want to get done and the order or priority to get them done. Although you may feel some tasks may have equal priority, still rate them in order or priority.

## Validate Your Task List with Key Stakeholders

Once your task list has been set and performance begins, it is important to validate your task list and sequencing. Two key stakeholders would be you immediate manager and family. Make sure at a minimum you run your task list by your immediate manager and your spouse. Your manager will appreciate this for two reasons.

First, this helps your manager you by laying out your prioritized work. Second, it shows them you are taking the initiative in managing your work. This is good for you because work priorities may change in a way only your manager can see, giving you first look at new or changing initiatives. Your spouse will appreciate this look because it includes them in allocating your time for your life together and joint goals. It also helps you reaffirm your own commitment to your higher goals. Validate your task list and task priorities with key people in your life, and do this regularly.

## Analyze Your Tasks for Viability

Analyze you task list for viability against your available resources. Do you have the time to do these tasks? Do you have the money, energy, and motivation to do these tasks? I am sure there are more questions that apply! Take a sober look at your task list and adjust in reality, not as a wish list. Carrying undone tasks week after week without action can be depressing and draining. Make a commitment to either complete them or drop them.

Over time, you will become much more thoughtful on your commitments and learn how to say no when you cannot fulfill them. In one week, I terminated five significant tasks after realizing I did not have the time or motivation to complete them. Disappointment is soon washed away with honestly dealing with commitments, and freeing up time to complete the important tasks, like writing this book!

## Revise, Re-Validate Your Task List Accordingly

Review, get feedback, and revise your task list and priorities regularly. Use the task list and priority validation process as an opportunity to get valuable feedback and build important relationships.

# 7

# QUEUES, ENGAGING, & DE-ENGAGING TASKS

## Creating Task Queues

A task queue is simply an intelligent informational database on a task. Although I recommend these queues created and maintained mostly by hand and stored in a folder, a computer database would be fine as this could be a "searchable" database.

The process of proper task switching requires referring to and updating task queues (Sohn & Anderson, 2003). Task queues can include information such as contact lists, task schedules, priorities, key tasks, what not to do and what to do, reference information such as scope of work, specifications, risks, issues, and analyses.

Review the topics below for suggestions of topics to include and then update in your task queues.

- Task objective
- Task sponsor, clients, and owner

- Stakeholders
- Key milestones and task schedule
- Task priorities
- Activities in process
- What to do on return to task
- Risks and mitigations
- Issues and resolutions
- Time and resources required
- Tasks to be deleted, delegated, transferred, shaved

Take the time to build quality task queues and then update and maintain them during the entire task completion cycle and even after the task is complete. Why after? Know tasks are rarely complete as you will most likely return to it or delegate the reopened task at a later time.

## Engaging Tasks

Again, eliminating undisciplined task switching improves task performance. This is because undisciplined task switching can be very harmful to your brain over time. Undisciplined task switching results in the unintended effect of confusion, poor performance, physiological brain damage. A more productive and efficient way to task switch is to engage and de-engage them.

Task engagement is the process of entering into a task prepared rather than unprepared. Engagement ensures you work on the appropriate task and eliminates noisy TUI. Engaging tasks properly requires referring to task queues, updating them, and gathering information with a bit of analysis on entry. Prerequisites for engagement are task prioritization and the creation of task queues.

Proper task engagement keeps you on track and efficient. Engagement keeps your priorities straight. First, task priorities have been determined and noted in your task queue. Second, engagement addresses key information before starting to ensure you are working the task with the proper assumptions. You will not have to search for a contact number, stakeholder, objective, or scope of work. You will not have to remember what to do first, who to contact, or who to include in a meeting. In short, you will become incredibly efficient in doing the right things and in proper order.

## Engage Tasks Better with an Action Plan

An Action Plan for your tasks creates a simple, yet powerful pathway to complete your tasks. A simple Action Plan is a one sheet summary of your task which can be very powerful in crystalizing your completion plan as well as communicating your plan and status to your team and stakeholders.

Using an Action Plan to manage tasks improves your ability to communicate task status to all stakeholders, achieve task goals, and complete tasks on time. The Action Plan template shown below includes the following information:

- Summary of the goal of the task

- Identified sponsor and client

- Summary of the scope of work

- Identified task team with contact and role information

- First 30 days of subtasks and actions

- Subtask and actions owners and due dates

- Issues and working resolutions

- Risks and proposed mitigations

- Task notes and reference information.

| Task Goal and Sponsor/Client | | | |
|---|---|---|---|
| | | | |

| Task Scope of Work | | | |
|---|---|---|---|
| | | | |

| Task Team | | | |
|---|---|---|---|
| | | | |

| Subtasks & Actions (30 Days) | | | |
|---|---|---|---|
| Subtask/Action | Due | Resp. | Status |
| | | | |
| | | | |
| | | | |
| | | | |
| | | | |
| | | | |
| | | | |
| | | | |
| | | | |

| Issues (Resolutions) & Risks (Mitigations) |
|---|
| Issue: _____. Resolution: <br> _____ |
| Risk: _____. Mitigation: <br> _____ |

| Notes & Reference information |
|---|
| |

# Action Plan Template

# De-Engaging Tasks

Task de-engagement is the process noting key information in the task file before switching off the task. This step is vital to enabling the brain to properly switch to the next task without retaining task residue or TUI from the previous task. In essence, de-engagement accomplishes two things. First, establishes a demarcation point between the "switched from" task and the "switched to" task. Second, it preserves key information on the "switched from" task that could be lost or hard to find when returning to the task.

The task file created for task engagement and de-engagement is similar to a medical record for a patient. All vital information is listed and carefully updated as information is added, deleted or changed. The figure below shows the proper work flow of the task engagement and de-engagement process. Note the demarcation lines between the tasks: the "De-engage" barriers. These barriers eliminate TUI and enable focus on one task at a time – highly effective task switching.

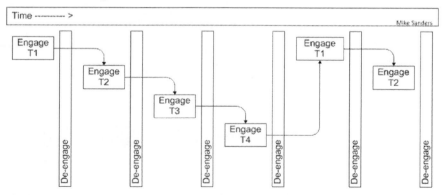

**Proper Task Switching - Engagement and De-Engagement (No TUI)**

De-engaging tasks places conscious barriers or demarcation walls between the tasks you are working on and the previous tasks. As a result, demarcation prevents intermittent switching, loss of focus, and emotional reactions to random thoughts. Addressing all these detractors produces better task performance and removes anxiety.

## Engaging and Ed-engaging is not an Option

We have a saying in Texas where I was born, "a quart jar holds a quart." This means when the brain becomes filled with information to its capacity, it starts dumping information to make room for more. If you de-engage your tasks properly, "you" control the dumping. If you do not, the "brain" will take care of that task for you. Left to the brain, important information may be dumped and not saved. I don't know about you, but I would like to control what is saved or dumped. And that is why de-engagement is so very important.

Do it and get more control of your information.

# REDUCE TASK LOAD

We all have more tasks than we can possibly complete. So we need a little bit of help. To reduce your task load, first list all of your tasks and then review them for four possibilities: delete, delegate, transfer, or shave (reducing) task scope.

## Delete Tasks

A task deleted is a task completed! The easiest way to complete a task is to not do it at all. This can be accomplished in several ways. First, prioritization will flush out the tasks that are not that important. Second, a good look at the tasks under the umbrella of your life goals will cull out even more tasks. Some tasks we do just because we like them, not because they add value. By the way, <u>fun</u> can be value! Just as long as we know why we are doing what we are doing, and the price we pay for doing one thing over another.

You will find it much easier to delete unnecessary tasks when you are in your analytical brain as opposed to your limbic brain. Decisions in task deletions will be easier when viewed through logic, resources available, and long-term goals.

## Delegate Tasks

Delegating tasks is one of the most important things we can do as managers and leaders (Wright State University). Yet why do we find delegating so hard to do? There are several reasons we do not like to delegate tasks.

- **We fear loss of power and control.** We may believe giving up the task will result in losing power or control. But this is far from the truth. Actually, effective task delegation requires we keep control over the work output. Decisions about how the task gets done are turned over to others. By delegating, we leverage the efforts of others to become more productive and influential. Delegating tasks frees up more time to complete other, more important tasks.

- **We think it takes too much time to train.** Our thinking here is this, in the time we take to train someone to perform the task we could have already completed the task. The fallacy in this logic is a task is rarely completed in the time we think it takes and similar tasks may come along that the training will also be appropriate for.

- **We want the task done now**. Patience is a virtue. Most of the time the task completion can wait and our compulsion to complete the task sooner is a preference, not a requirement.

- **We don't like or trust the delegate**. We question if the delegatee will do the task correctly due to trust or personality issues, but not reality. We question the delegate's commitment or sense of urgency and desire to do a good job.

- **We think we can do it better**. Our pride may get in the way of good judgment. There may be many ways to complete a task. And we can always learn better and faster ways to work. Losing our pride, opening our minds eventually equates to continual improvement. If we truly care about what is done and improvement, we will open our minds to better ways to work and understand tasks can always be done better.

- **We fear the delegate may point out flaws in our own process**. Transparency in task management is important for improvement. What we want as a task delegator is just the opposite of confirmation of a process – we want the delegate to point out flaws. This is one of the major objectives of the delegation.

- **We identify with the task**. Doing this task may seem like a signature experience for us. However, we need to put all tasks we do in context of our higher goals and limited resources.

- **We feel doing the task gives us visibility**. Doing this task may provide high-level visibility for us. However, again we need to put all tasks we do in context of our higher goals and limited resources.

- **We believe if we delegate the task, we may not be needed anymore**. The fear of losing our need for being important or needed, or our desire to keep the task for job security may cause us to hold on to tasks. The objective though is to ensure we have the time to perform the key tasks on our list. Weigh fears of job security or dependency against the success of completing priorities.

Whatever the reason to hang onto tasks, we need to delegate much more to enable time, make space for us to do the important things in our lives and handle key tasks on our priority list.

## Transfer Tasks

Evaluate your tasks for work properly performed by others or other groups. When candidate tasks for transfer are identified, several considerations must be made. Will this transfer require a costly confrontation or meet with severe resistance? Will the transfer reduce your authority or put your job position in jeopardy? Does the task give you visibility or power and control you may require to perform other tasks? And would the loss of this task represent a perceived lack of authority, initiative, or status?

These questions may be reasons to either transfer or keep a task. But they should be addressed honestly to understand the costs of keeping or transferring the task.

## Shave (Reduce) Task Scope

If task deletion, delegation, or transfer is not possible, shaving or reducing task scope is the last option to address your task load. To reduce task scope, list all actions required to complete the task and review each subtask in the process for value. The best approach is to first create a flow chart of all subtasks as shown in the diagram below.

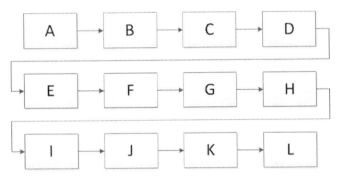

**Original Subtask Process Flow**

Identify all non-value-added subtasks in the process flow. Non-value added tasks may be those that are not essential or discretionary.

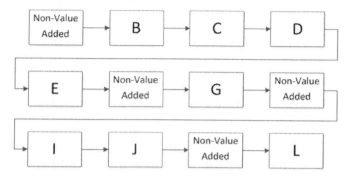

**Non-Value-Added Subtasks are Identified**

Delete the non-value-added tasks from the task flow. The task scope has now been shaved or reduced as shown below. The newly formed task will take less time to complete allowing you more time for other tasks.

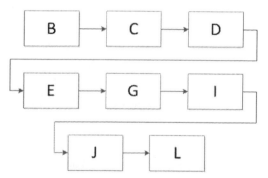

**Task with Reduced Scope**

## Skills to Reduce Task Load

Any of the four tools discussed above to reduce task load most likely will require dealing with others. For instance, you may need to negotiate the deletion of a task with a manager or client. You may need to exercise delegation skills to assign to others. You may need to deal with conflict when transferring tasks to others reluctant to take on the tasks. And finally, you will need to use analytical skills to shave (reduce) task scope.

As a result, you should acquire or hone the skills required to support task load reduction including:

- Negotiation
- Delegation
- Business Writing
- Conflict Management
- Interpersonal
- Project Management
- Analysis/Logic
- Time Management
- Presentation

# 9

# GET FEEDBACK, ACT ON IT

As you use the Advanced Multitasking process, it is important to ask your stakeholders how you are doing. Stakeholders include key business associates, your management, vendors, clients, family and friends how you are doing. The idea is to get feedback for improvement in task management. Topics include feedback on task priorities, living up to your commitments, performance quality, timeliness, service, interpersonal skills, and resources.

## Validate Your Task List and Task Priorities

Once your task list has been set and performance begins, it is important to validate your task list and sequencing with stakeholders. Two key stakeholders would be you immediate manager and family. Make sure at a minimum you run your task list by your immediate manager and your spouse. Your manager will appreciate this for two reasons.

First, it helps your manager you by laying out your prioritized work. Second, it shows them you are taking the initiative in managing your work. This is good for you because work priorities may change in a way only your manager can see, giving you first look at new or changing initiatives.

Second, your spouse will appreciate this task validation because it includes him or her in the process of allocating your time for your life together, your joint goals.

Third, it also helps you reaffirm your commitment to your higher goals. Validate your task list and task priorities with key people in your life, and do this regularly.

## Analyze Your Task List for Viability

Analyze you task list for viability against your available resources. Do you have the time to do these tasks? Do you have the money to do these tasks? Do you have the skills and energy to do these tasks? I am sure there are more questions that apply including inclination! Take a sober look at your task list and adjust for reality, not simply a wish list. Carrying undone tasks week after week without action can be depressing and draining. Make a commitment to either do them or drop them. Be honest with yourself and those who depend on you.

Over time, you will become more stingy with your time and learn how to say "no" to commitments when you cannot possibly fulfill them. In one week alone I terminated five significant tasks after realizing I did not have the time to do them. The disappointment of those benefiting from the tasks was soon forgotten with the admission I did not have time to complete the tasks. This not only took a load off my mind, but freed me up to complete the tasks important to me, including this book.

## Practice Continual Improvement

It is important once we ask others for feedback, we act on it. There are a couple of reasons for this. Tasking feedback is a time-dated opportunity to act. That is, comments from others have a shelf life affecting both applicability to the tasking process and the relationship with those who gave the feedback.

Act swiftly and without bias or defensiveness to make the most progress. Get back to those who give you feedback about how you used their comments to make improvements. During the improvement cycle, open your mind to change, knowing that if it is uncomfortable, you are probably making good progress.

Feedback received on your new tasking model is an opportunity to develop rich relationships with your co-workers, management, clients, vendors, family and friends. Use the opportunity often and with the intent to act on feedback received. You will get what you give.

# 10

# WHY ADVANCED MULTITASKING?

## Advanced Multitasking versus Multitasking

As shown in the figure below, unrestrained task switching produces an overwhelming and confusing view of our task day. This dilutes our focus and produces the opposite of the intended effect of productivity – slow task performance, brain freeze, mistakes and incompletion.

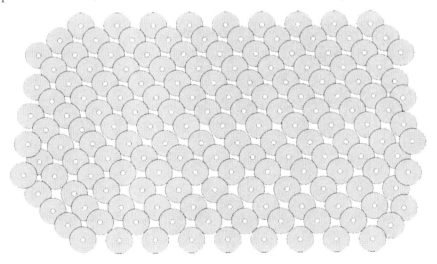

## The Multitasking Illusion – Reflexive Task Switching

# We end up doing less and hurting our brain.

What we do to ourselves when we try to multitask results in the exact opposite of our intention to do more. We end up doing less and hurting our brain. As an added extra, we also drift away from reaching our goals.

The Advanced Multitasking approach is not really multitasking at all. This simple tasking system would be better named serial tasking or multiple task management. Instead of falling prey to the winds of short-term, poorly prioritized task selection from emotional moments, the Advanced Multitasking model prepares us for intelligent, high-level, self-determined task engagement.

We affectively see only one task at a time, much like a PEZ® dispenser as shown in the figure below. This is an extremely effective answer to focused working in our noisy, fast-paced, distracting environment.

**Serial Task Switching – Focusing on One Task at a Time**

The beauty of Advanced Multitasking is in its simplicity. This tasking system, done well, is constructed manually by you and costs you absolutely nothing – except for a small investment in planning time and task engagement maintenance. This relatively small amount of effort is paid back in huge dividends, indefinitely. Not a bad return-on-investment.

# 11

# DRINK MORE WATER

Drink a lot of water.

Your brain is composed of over 70% water. To maintain and even improve thinking power, you need to keep your brain properly hydrated. A dehydrated brain can lead to memory loss, headaches, drowsiness, and impaired analytical 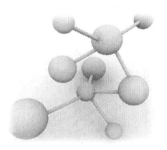 and critical-thinking ability (Gown, 2010; Popkin, D'Anci, & Rosenberg, 2010).

For these reasons, drink a lot of water.

## Calculating the Water Drinking Quota

How much water should we drink? A good rule of thumb is the number of ounces of water you need to drink each day is equal to your weight in pounds divided by two.

For instance, for those weighing 160 pounds, the daily water quota would be 160 ÷ 2, or 80 ounces of water. Since there are 128 ounces of water per gallon, 80 ounces would be about two thirds of a gallon, or about 2 1/2 quarts (32 ounces per quart).

Note doctors recommend drinking eight, eight-ounce glasses of water per day – or 64 ounces. However, this amount would be appropriate only for someone with a weight of about 130 pounds or less.

## Drink the Daily Water Quota

Do the math for yourself and drink at least your quota each day. No matter what, drink a good amount of water every day. And know the water drinking quota cannot be achieved by drinking other liquids such as coffee, tea, soda, alcohol, or fruit juice. Actually, alcohol is a dehydrator. This explains why you may get a headache from a hangover – your brain is dehydrated and it hurts!

So if you drink alcohol, drink twice the amount of water at a minimum to combat any dehydration. This also helps you maintain your ability to do critical thinking and may even stave off a hangover.

## *Water Types*

Regarding what water to drink, there are many water products to choose from. These include bottled water, home-filtered tap water, reverse osmosis, chemical additives to water, and hydrolyzing systems. Of these, I recommend drinking water made from the hydrolysis process. Hydrolyzed water is more absorbent, hydrating your body better, because it produces water with smaller $H_2O$ molecule clusters. This hydration is better both in terms of amount of water absorbed and the speed of absorption. Hydrolyzed water is also alkaline which is considered better for your general health.

## Bottled Water

Try to stay away from bottled water. Even expensive bottled water can be acidic, not considered good for your general health, and may have absorbed leached plastic from its container – this also not good for you. Bottled water may have been in its plastic container for over a year and  can be exposed to very high temperatures during its transportation. Both the length of time in the container and high temperatures are a prescription for plastic leaching into the water.

# 12

## WHAT'S NEXT?

## Important is simple.

Knowing and living this can greatly improve what you do, how you do what you do, and your success in doing it. The Advanced Multitasking model is a holistic approach to task management. It starts asking you to answer the question, "what do I want?" It would have you practice cognitive thinking in your four brains – preferably in your pre-frontal cortex or non-conscious brain when planning or making big decisions. It would have you list and prioritize all tasks – personal and business, and then validate that list with key people in your life – your stakeholders.

Finally, the model asks you to create task queues or knowledge repositories for holding vital task information. These queues can be thought of as "thought banks" to save evolving task knowledge as you work through your day.

Then you begin.

Engage. And as you leave a task, you do not switch, but de-engage, saving all vital information into your queues, and preventing that disabling TUI. The engagement process allows your focus to remain keenly on the task at hand. De-engaging also constrains anxiety, as can be assured all vital information is saved and out of your head.

As time permits, you practice task load management. That is, eliminate tasks and reduce scope. Knowing you cannot possibly do everything you want to do, task load management, or DDTSs, can help reduce the mountain of work that can disable you in the long term. Delete, delegate, transfer, and shave (reduce) task scope. This saves time and energy for your important work.

Using a planner is vital to task management as it allows you to quietly reflect on all your work and tap into deeper pools of conscious thinking through visualization and muscle memory. A planner, used for all tasks, has the synergistic effect of task cross-talk – enabling you to review all your priorities visually. I call my planner the "book of miracles" since I believe anything in my planner gets done.

You get feedback on your progress from key stakeholders regularly because you need an objective view of your work to make it whole and to improve. This also aids in buy-in from the important people in your life.

And when you are done with all of this, you start all over again. Over time, the Advanced Multitasking model loses its label of hard work, and becomes a welcome and empowering friend in a world of seemingly uncharted chaos, powerlessness, and confusion.

# You can't do everything.

You can do a lot, but not everything. This means you need to make important choices about what you do, and what you don't do. Your tasks define you. So task selections are important. Advanced Multitasking helps you determine what is important and what you have control over. Done right, the intersection of both become your tasks.

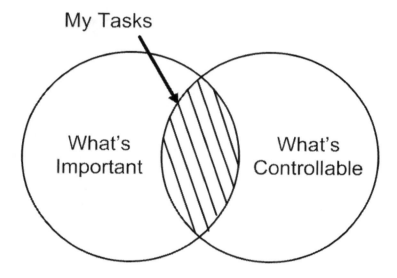

Don't just fall into tasks by pleasing others, from sloppy or impulsive thinking, or guilt. This is your life. Please choose your tasks wisely.

The very best to you.

# REFERENCES

Altmann, E. M. (2004a). The preparation effect in task switching: Carryover of SOA. *Memory & Cognition, 32,* 153-163.

Altmann, E. M. (2004b). Advance preparation in task switching: What work is being done? *Psychological Science, 15,* 616–622.

Altmann, E. M. (2006). Task switching is not cue switching. *Psychonomic Bulletin & Review, 13,* 1016–1022.

Altmann, E. M., & Gray, W. D. (2002). Forgetting to remember: The functional relationship of decay and interference. *Psychological Science, 13,* 27–33.

Altmann, E. M., & Trafton, J. G. (2002). Memory for goals: An activation-based model. *Cognitive Science, 26,* 39–83.

Alvino, G. (2007). Body: The intelligence of the body in renewing itself daily. *Heart to Heart Associates.* Retrieved from *http://www.hearttoheartassociates.com/miracle-body.htm*

Anderson, J. R. (1993). *Rules of the Mind.* Hillsdale, NJ: Erlbaum.

Anderson, J. R., & Lebiere, C. (Eds.). (1998). *The atomic components of thought.* Hillsdale, NJ: Erlbaum.

Arbuthnott, K. D. (2005). The influence of cue type on backward inhibition. Journal of *Experimental Psychology: Learning, Memory, and Cognition, 31,* 1030–1042.

Arrington, C. M., & Logan, G. D. (2004). Episodic and semantic components of the compound-stimulus strategy in the explicit task-cuing procedure. *Memory & Cognition, 32,* 965–978.

Avery-Snell, J. (2007, June 19). Is Multi-tasking Counterproductive? *American Management Association.* Retrieved from *http://www.amanet.org/training/articles/Is-Multi-tasking-Counterproductive.aspx*

Baddeley, A. D. (1986). *Working Memory.* Oxford, England: Oxford University Press.

Baddeley, A. D., & Scott, D. (1971). Short term forgetting in the absence of proactive interference. *Quarterly Journal of Experimental Psychology, 23,* 275–283.

Borst, J., & Taatgen, N. (2007). The costs of multitasking in threaded cognition. *Carnegie Melon University Press – Department of Psychology.* Pittsburgh, PA: Carnegie Melon University.

Comaford, C. (2012, April 4). Got inner peace? 5 ways to get it now. *Forbes.com.* Retrieved from *http://www.forbes.com/sites/christinecomaford/2012/04/04/got-inner-peace-5-ways-to-get-it-now/*

CareerBuilder. (2011, July 28). Nearly half of employers say workers are burned out on their jobs. CareerBuilder.com. Retrieved from http://www.techjournal.org/2011/07/nearly-half-of-employers-say-workers-are-burned-out-on-their-jobs/

Casteneda, C. (1968). *The teachings of Don Juan: A Yaqui way of knowledge.* Berkeley, CA: University of California Press.

Clark, D. (2010, September 24). The Hawthorne Effect. *NwLink.com.* Retrieved from *http://www.nwlink.com/~donclark/hrd/history/hawthorne.html*

Dvorsky, G. (2007, March 19). Managing your 50,000 daily thoughts. *SentientThoughts.com.* Retrieved from *http://www.sentientdevelopments.com/2007/03/managing-your-50000-daily-thoughts.html*

Dictionary of Sociology (1998). The Hawthorne Effect. Retrieved from *http://www.encyclopedia.com/topic/Hawthorne_effect.aspx#1-1O88:Hawthornestudies-full*

Economist. (2008, November 3). The Hawthorne effect. *The Economist.* Retrieved from *http://www.economist.com/node/12510632*

Estes, W. K. (1955). Statistical theory of spontaneous recovery and regression. *Psychological Review, 62,* 145–154.

Fagot, C. D. (1994). *Chronometric investigations of task switching.* Ph.D. thesis, Psychology Department, University of California, San Diego.

FixQuotes. (N.D.). Publilius Syrus. *FixQuotes.com.* Retrieved from *http://fixquotes.com/authors/publilius-syrus.htm*

Franke, R. H. & Kaul, J. D. (1978). The Hawthorne experiments: First statistical interpretation. *American Sociological Review, 43,* 623-643.

Gerhand, S. (1999). The prefrontal cortex - executive and cognitive functions. *Oxford Journals*. Retrieved from *http://brain.oxfordjournals.org/content/122/5/994.full*

Gopher, D., Armony, L., & Greenspan, Y. (2000). Switching tasks and attention policies. *Journal of Experimental Psychology: General, 129,* 308-229.

Gown, J. (2010, October 15). Why your brain needs water. *Psychology Today*. Retrieved from *http://www.psychologytoday.com/blog/you-illuminated/201010/why-your-brain-needs-water*

Hawthorne, J. (2009). Change your thoughts, change your world. *Jennifer Read Hawthorne*. Retrieved from *http://www.jenniferhawthorne.com/articles/change_your_t houghts.html*

Jarrehult, B. (2012). Can multitasking result in more than 60 percent longer project time? *Innovation Management*. Retrieved from *http://www.innovationmanagement.se/2012/08/14/can-multi-tasking-result-in-more-than-60-longer-project-time/*

Kieras, D. E., Meyer, D. E., Ballas, J. A., & Lauber, E. J. (2000). Modern computational perspectives on executive mental processes and cognitive control: Where to from here? In S. Monsell & J. Driver (eds.) *Control of Cognitive Processes: Attention and Performance XVIII,* 681-712. Cambridge, MA: M.I.T. Press.

Kleiman, J. (2013, January 15). How multitasking hurts your brain (and your effectiveness at work). *Forbes*. Retrieved from http://www.forbes.com/sites/work-in-progress/2013/01/15/how-multitasking-hurts-your-brain-and-your-effectiveness-at-work/

Koch, C. (2009, February/March). Measure more, argue less. *Scientific American Mind.* Retrieved from *http://www.readcube.com/articles/10.1038/scientificameric anmind0209-16?locale=en*

Koch, I. (2005). Sequential task predictability in task switching. *Psychonomic Bulletin & Review, 12,* 107-112.

Kramer, A. F., Hahn, S.,& Gopher, D. (1999). Task coordination and aging: explorations of executive control processes in the task switching paradigm. *Acta Psychologica, 101,* 339–378.

Logan, G. D., & Bundesen, C. (2003). Clever homunculus: Is there an endogenous act of control in the explicit task-cuing procedure*? Journal of Experimental Psychology: Human Perception and Performance, 29,* 575–599.

Logan, G. D., & Bundesen, C. (2004). Very clever homunculus: Compound stimulus strategies for the explicit task-cuing procedure. *Psychonomic Bulletin & Review, 11,* 832–840.

Logan, G. D., & Schneider, D. W. (2006). Interpreting instructional cues in task switching procedures: The role of mediator retrieval. *Journal of Experimental Psychology: Learning, Memory, and Cognition, 32,* 347–363.

Luce, R. D. (1986). *Response times: their role in inferring elementary mental organization.* New York: Oxford University Press.

Mayr, U. & Kliegl, R. (2000). Task-set switching and long-term memory retrieval. *Journal of Experimental Psychology: Learning, Memory, and Cognition, 26,* 1124-1140.

Mayr, U. (2006). What matters in the cued task-switching paradigm: Tasks or cues? *Psychonomic Bulletin & Review, 13,* 794–799.

Merriam-Webster. (2014). Multitasking. *Merriam-Webster.com.* Retrieved from *http://www.merriam-webster.com/dictionary/multitasking*

Meuter, R. F. I. & Allport, A. (1999). Bilingual language switching in naming: Asymmetrical costs of language selection. *Journal of Memory and Language, 40*(1), 25-40.

Meyer, D. E. & Kieras, D. E. (1997a). EPIC - A computational theory of executive cognitive processes and multiple-task performance: Part 1. Basic mechanisms. *Psychological Review, 104,* 3-65.

Meyer, D. E. & Kieras, D. E. (1997b). A computational theory of executive cognitive processes and multiple-task performance: Part 2. Accounts of psychological refractory-period phenomena. *Psychological Review, 104,* 749-791.

Monsell, S., Yeung, N., & Azuma, R. (2000). Reconfiguration of task-set: Is it easier to switch to the weaker task? *Psychological Research, 63,* 250-264.

Monsell, S., & Mizon, G. A. (2006). Can the task-cuing paradigm measure an "endogenous" task-set reconfiguration process? *Journal of Experimental Psychology: Human Perception and Performance, 32,* 493–516.

Philipp, A. M., & Koch, I. (2006). Task inhibition and task repetition in task switching. *European Journal of Cognitive Psychology, 18,* 624–639.

Popkin, B. M., D'Anci, K. E. & Rosenberg, I. H. (2010, August). Water, hydration, and health. *US National Library of Sciences.* Retrieved from *http://www.ncbi.nlm.nih.gov/pmc/articles/PMC2908954/*

Posen, R. (2012, October 19). How to use your time wisely by prioritizing your goals. *Entrepreneur.com.* Retrieved from *http://www.entrepreneur.com/article/224675*

Psychology Matters. (N.D.) Multitasking - Switching Costs - Subtle switching costs cut efficiency, raise risk. *APA Online - Psychology Matters.* Retrieved from *http://www.apa.org/research/action/multitask.aspx*

Rogers, R., & Monsell, S. (1995). Costs of a predictable switch between simple cognitive tasks. *Journal of Experimental Psychology: General, 124,* 207–231.

Rubenstein, J., Mayer, D, & Evans, J. (2001, August 5). Is multitasking more efficient? Shifting mental gears costs time, especially when shifting to less familiar tasks. *Journal of Experimental Psychology.* Retrieved from *http://apa.org/news/press/releases/2001/08/multitasking.aspx*

Rubenstein, J., Mayer, D, & Evans, J. (2001). Executive Control of Cognitive Processes in Task Switching. *Journal of Experimental Psychology - Human Perception and Performance, 27*(4).

Shier, D., Butler, J., & Lewis, R. (2013). *Hole's human anatomy and physiology (13th Ed).* Columbus, OH: McGraw-Hill Education.

Schneider, D. W., & Logan, G. D. (2005). Modeling task switching without switching tasks: A short-term priming account of explicitly cued performance. *Journal of Experimental Psychology: General, 134,* 343–367.

Schneider, D. W., & Logan, G. D. (2007). Task switching versus cue switching: Using transition cuing to disentangle sequential effects in task-switching performance. *Journal of Experimental Psychology: Learning, Memory, and Cognition, 33*, 370–378.

Schuch, S., & Koch, I. (2003). The role of response selection for inhibition of task sets in task shifting. *Journal of Experimental Psychology: Human Perception and Performance, 29*, 92–105.

Smith, D. (2001, October). Multitasking undermines our efficiency, study suggests. *Monitor on Psychology. 32 (9)* 13. Retrieved from *http://www.apa.org/monitor/oct01/multitask.aspx*

Sohn, M. H., & Anderson, J. R. (2003). Stimulus related priming during task switching. *Memory & Cognition, 31*, 775-780.

The Quotations Page. (N.D.). Publilius Syrus quotations. *TheQuotationsPage.com*. Retrieved from http://www.quotationspage.com/quotes/Publilius_Syrus

Waller, M. (2004). *The Dance of the Lion and the Unicorn*. Bloomington, Indiana, AuthorHouse.

Wazack, F., Homel, B., & Allport, A. (2003). Task-switching and long-term priming: Role of episodic stimulus-task bindings in task shift costs. *Cognitive Psychology, 46*, 361-413.

Wechsler, B. (2006, September 22). Consciousness is weak. *Ezine Articles*. Retrieved from *http://ezinearticles.com/?Consciousness-is-Weak&id=307545*.

Weinschenk, S. (2012, September 18). The true cost of multi-tasking. *Psychology Today*. Retrieved from *http://www.psychologytoday.com/blog/brain-wise/201209/the-true-cost-multi-tasking*

Wickelgren, W. A. (1977). Speed-accuracy tradeoff and information processing dynamics. *Acta Psychologica, 41,* 67–85.

Wright State University. (N.D.). Delegating strategically. *Wright.edu.* Retrieved from *http://www.wright.edu~scott.williams/LeaderLetter/delegating.ht m*

Yeung, N. & Monsell, S. (2003). Switching between tasks of unequal familiarity: The role of stimulus-attribute and response-set selection. *Journal of Experimental Psychology-Human Perception and Performance, 29*(2), 455-469.

# SEMINARS BY MIKE

Advanced Multitasking

Beyond Emotional Intelligence

Controlling Communication Channels

Rise of the Knowledge Worker

Power Networking

SuperConnectivity

Business Writing

In-Sizing

Mike Sanders is a public speaker, author, instructor, project manager, technical writer, and Native American. He has spoken at over 100 business and corporate events throughout California and Nevada. Venues include business associations, conferences and symposiums, universities, and corporate and government organizations.

Contact Mike if you are interested in having him speak at your event or organization at mike@mike-sanders.com or call 714-615-5477.

# CONTACT INFORMATION

www.advanced-multitasking.com

info@advanced-multitasking.com

mike@mike-sanders.com

www.mike-sanders.com

(714) 615-5477

## Mike Sanders

2913 El Camino Real, No. 432

Tustin, CA. 92782

Made in the USA
Charleston, SC
25 June 2015